D0457173

Churchill County Library
553 S. Maine Street
Fallon, Nevada 89406
(775) 423-7581

KINGFISHER READERS

level 2

Where Animals Live

Brenda Stones and
Thea Feldman

KINGFISHER

NEW YORK

KINGFISHER
LONDON & NEW YORK

Copyright © Kingfisher 2012
Published in the United States by Kingfisher,
175 Fifth Ave., New York, NY 10010
Kingfisher is an imprint of Macmillan Children's Books, London.
All rights reserved.

Distributed in the U.S. and Canada by Macmillan,
175 Fifth Ave., New York, NY 10010

Library of Congress Cataloging-in-Publication data
has been applied for.

Series editor: Thea Feldman
Literacy consultant: Ellie Costa, Bank St. College, New York

ISBN: 978-0-7534-6877-7 (HB)
ISBN: 978-0-7534-6878-4 (PB)

Kingfisher books are available for special promotions
and premiums. For details contact: Special Markets
Department, Macmillan, 175 Fifth Ave., New York, NY 10010.

For more information, please visit
www.kingfisherbooks.com

Printed in China
9 8 7 6 5 4 3 2 1
1TR/0712/UG/WKT/105MA

Picture credits
The Publisher would like to thank the following for permission to reproduce their material. Every care has
been taken to trace copyright holders. However, if there have been unintentional omissions or failure to trace
copyright holders, we apologize and will, if informed, endeavor to make corrections in any future edition.
Top = t; Bottom = b; Center = c; Left = l; Right = r
Cover Shutterstock (SS)/RCPPHOTO; Pages 4 SS/Pichuigin Dmitry; 5t SS/Jill Battglio; 5b SS/Hannamariah;
6–7 Photolibrary; 7 FLPA/Yva Momatiuk & John Eastcott; 8 SS/Nik Nikiz; 9 FLPA/ZSSD/Minden; 10 FLPA/
Panada Photo; 11 SS/Vladimir Chernyansky; 12–13 SS/MTrebbin; 13t SS/Tramper; 14–15 SS/alterfalter;
15 SS/Kristof Degreef; 16 SS/Robert Hackett; 17t SS/Anne Kitzman; 17b FLPA/Imagebroker; 18t SS/Johan
Sanepoel; 18b SS/Four Oaks; 19 SS/Joy Brown; 20 Nature PL/Kim Taylor; 21 SS/Krisvosheev Vitaly;
22 SS/Mikhail Olykainan; 23 Alamy/Chris Howes; 24 SS/janr34; 25t SS/Studiotouch; 25b SS/Indric;
26–27 Photolibrary; 27 SS/Cathy Keifer; 28 Photolibrary; 29 Photolibrary/Usher D; 30 SS/Graham Taylor;
31t Alamy/Kevin Foy; 31b SS/RCPPHOTO.

Contents

Home, sweet home!

Every wild animal needs
a place to live.

The place an animal lives
is called a **habitat**.

A habitat is an animal's home.

A seal's home is by the sea.

Some animals
live in **nests**
in trees.

Some animals
live underground.

Let's visit
more animals
at home!

Penguins

The South Pole is the coldest place on Earth.

But many penguins live there.

Special feathers keep them warm in the water and on land.

Penguins lay eggs on land.

The father Emperor penguin
balances the egg on his feet.

It stays warm there
until it hatches.

Polar bears

The North Pole is very cold too.

Polar bears live there.

Big paws help them walk on ice.

A polar bear digs a **snow den** before she gives birth to cubs.

Snow packed around the den keeps everyone warm and cozy!

Foxes

Where do foxes live?

They live in fields and woods.

But you might not see them.

They sleep during the day.

Foxes hunt for food at night.

Sometimes they come into towns
to look for food.

You might see one then.

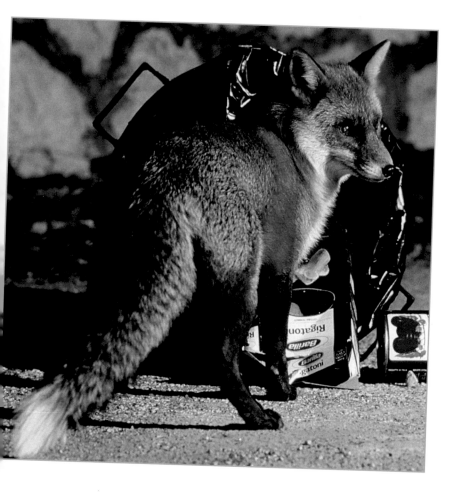

Moles

Look at these piles of dirt.

Where did they come from?

From a mole's home!

A mole lives underground.

He digs his home, and tunnels too.

A mole's home is called a **burrow**.

How does a mole dig a burrow?

With his sharp claws and teeth.

Chimpanzees

Many animals spend time high above the ground.

Chimpanzees sleep in nests in trees in forests in Africa.

A chimp learns to build a nest when she is young.

Chimps build new nests every night.

Squirrels

Squirrels live in trees too.

They live in woods, parks,
and gardens.

A squirrel climbs
a tree with
her sharp claws.

Her tail helps
her to balance.

A squirrel builds
a nest in a tree too.

It is called a **drey**.

A drey is made of
twigs, leaves,
and warm **moss**.

Baby squirrels sleeping in a drey

Bird nests

Many birds build nests
when it is time to
lay eggs.

The weaverbird
is named for
the amazing nests
it weaves from
leaves.

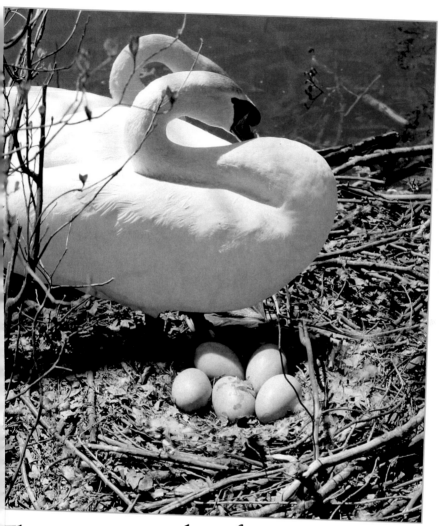

This swan nest has five eggs.

The mother will sit on the eggs.

The father will chase away other animals.

Swallows

Some animals live in two places.

This swallow lives in one place when the weather is warm.

When it gets cold she flies away.

She flies to her second home.

It is in a warmer place.

Every summer the swallow flies
back to her first home.

She comes back to the same nest!

Ants

Many ants build a home together.

It is made of sticks and leaves.

It is called an **anthill**.

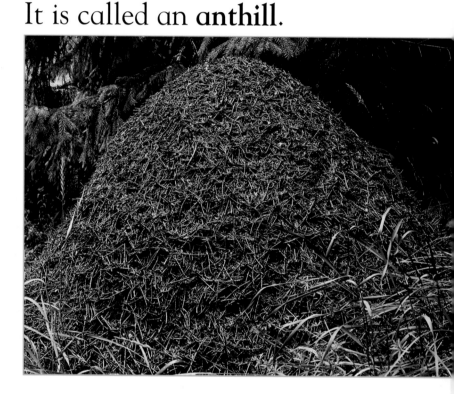

Thousands of ants
can live together
in one anthill!

Wasps

Wasps build a home
together too.

They build a nest from
chewed bits of wood.

The nest is very strong.

The queen wasp lays eggs
in the nest.

Other wasps take care of the nest
and the eggs.

Butterflies

Butterflies seem so free!

But they need places to live too.

They live in places with flowers, such as fields and gardens.

Butterflies get food from flowers.

A butterfly lays eggs
right on the leaves of plants!

Caterpillars grow in the eggs.

They hatch and stay on the leaves.

Spiders

Spiders live everywhere except in Antarctica.

Some spiders spin **webs**, but a web is not a home.

It is a trap to catch food!

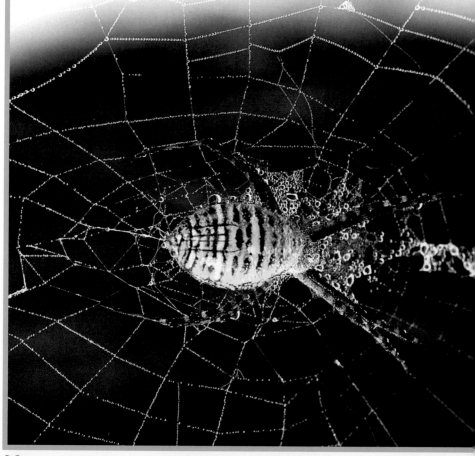

Spiderwebs can be
many different
shapes and sizes.

Safe at home

Wild animals live in many places.

They live in and by the sea.

They live in cold places.

They live in forests, parks, gardens, fields, and elsewhere.

It is up to us to take care
of all these places.

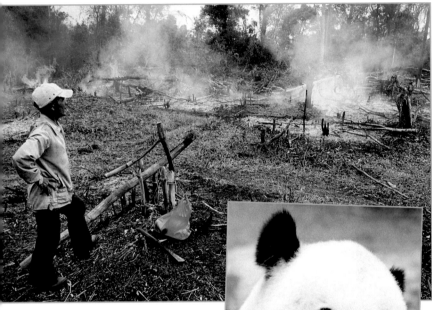

We need to
keep habitats safe
for animals
wherever
they live!

Glossary

anthill the home that many ants build together

burrow an underground home for some animals such as moles

drey the nest a squirrel builds in a tree

habitat the natural home for a wild animal

moss a kind of green plant that squirrels use in their nests

nests homes where some animals, such as squirrels, swallows, swans, and wasps, may live and raise young; also places chimpanzees build to sleep in each night

snow den a home dug in the snow

webs traps that some spiders spin to catch food